KNOWN
BY
Name

RAHAB

Don't Judge Me,
God Says I'm

Qualified

STUDY GUIDE | FOUR SESSIONS

Kasey Van Norman, Jada Edwards,
Nicole Johnson

With Karen Lee-Thorp

Har
Res

T0182266

Known by Name: Rahab
© 2019 by Kasey Van Norman, Jada Edwards, and Nicole Johnson

Requests for information should be addressed to:
HarperChristian Resources, 3900 Sparks Dr. SE, Grand Rapids, Michigan 49546

ISBN 978-0-310-09631-3 (softcover)
ISBN 978-0-310-09632-0 (ebook)

Cover image: © *LanaBrest/Shutterstock*
Interior design: Denise Froehlich

First Printing November 2018 / Printed in the United States of America

Contents

How This Study

Works

Rahab: Girl Boss

Do you love everything about yourself, or are there things in your past or present that you criticize yourself for? Do you feel like others are judging you? Do you feel like you're not worth anything to God? If you struggle with these questions, then you have something in common with a woman in the Bible: Rahab.

Rahab's story is the story of a girl boss. She was assertive, confident, a woman doing what she had to do to support her family. But her identity was shaped by her environment and upbringing. She didn't have a Bible study to attend or a podcast to download because she grew up in a culture that believed in many gods, not God. A highly sexualized, anti-God society. But one day two strangers knocked on her door, and she glimpsed the possibility of a better life. She chose to believe in a God that she'd only heard stories about. Her legacy became an example of what happens when we as women trust our intuition about what God says about us, not what the world says about us. Through her story we can learn to shed those unhelpful labels that others put on us, and those fears that we have in our own hearts, and revel in God's unconditional love.

Rahab: Don't Judge Me, God Says I'm Qualified is a study for women who want to get into the real, messy parts of our lives that are usually under wraps. Through video of a Bible teacher, a Christian counselor, and an actor playing out present-day dramas, we will explore first the human perspective: how Rahab felt, how she saw herself, and how others saw her, as well as how we see ourselves. We will also discover God's perspective: how he sees Rahab and how he sees us. We will find our own stories in the pages of Scripture.

A Typical Session

A session of the study will go like this:

Check In. In Session 1 you'll introduce yourselves. In later sessions you'll have a chance to share something you discovered about yourself in-between sessions.

At a Glance: Rahab. This is a quick snapshot of an age-old problem we still deal with today, Rahab's age-old solution or mistake, and a taste of God's wisdom on the subject.

Watch The Video. Each video segment is 20–25 minutes long. It opens with a drama and then moves into a fast-paced teaching. Session 1 begins with all three of the presenters together, talking about the theme of the series. This study guide contains space for you to take notes on what you see in the video.

Group Discussion. The heart of the study is your conversation with the other women in your group. You'll be talking mainly about the real experiences of your lives. However, because this isn't group therapy, we strongly recommend that you commit yourself to the group ground rules discussed below.

Closing Prayer. End with your group leader or a volunteer reading aloud the prayer suggested in this section. Of course, any offered prayer is acceptable.

Keep This Close. These are a few short, memorable lines from the video that you may want to copy into your phone to go back to during the week.

On Your Own. Finally, you'll find five or six activities you can select from to carry your exploration of the topic deeper during the week. There is one verse of Scripture you can memorize and come back to over the remaining sessions of the study. There are journaling ideas. You can read Rahab's story in the Bible. You can pray or reflect on the drama. Do whichever of these activities you find helpful. Don't feel pressure to do more than you have time for. You'll have a chance to share something you got out of these activities when your group gathers next time. You'll also have a chance to recite your memory verse together.

Group Ground Rules

This study gives you more of an opportunity to open up about your real life than most studies. You won't be pushed, but you will be invited, to talk about how you see yourself and how you live. But your group is not a therapy session. It's not led by a counselor. If you need professional counseling or a forum to share the story of your past, ask your group leader or church leaders to recommend resources.

The following ground rules will help you stay on track. You should go over them in your first meeting to be sure that everyone understands and agrees.

Confidentiality. Everything shared in the group must stay in the group. Don't repeat to outsiders what others share, even if you are all friends. If a group member misses a meeting, don't bring her up to date by sharing what others said in her absence. If something happens in the group that upsets you, don't discuss it with someone outside your group. Go to your group leader.

Disclosure. This should be a safe place to tell the group the difficult truths of your past. However, the group does not need all the ugly details. Give your group the four-or five-sentence summary of your situation. If you need someone to hear the whole story, ask your group leader to help you get connected with a counselor. She can help you find the person on your church staff who has the names of counselors in your area.

Tears. It's often good to cry when you share something hard. You're not embarrassing the group. If someone in your group cries, avoid words and actions that attempt to fix her sadness or solve her problem. Comfort is good; fixing is not. Don't let tears derail your time together. Keep going. The woman who has tears will be better sooner if the conversation carries on.

Shared Airtime. Everyone in the group needs an equal chance to talk. Avoid telling long stories, especially about your past or about what you are struggling with today. If you have a lot on your mind that needs to be said, ask your group leader to help you get connected with a counselor.

Present Orientation. Rahab's past will come up in the study, and you'll have some time to think about your past. But for group discussion, concentrate on talking about who you are today, shaped by your past, but not living in the past. Don't ask the group to sit through an account of what you went through. That's for counseling.

Advice. Avoid giving advice to other group members. If someone reveals a problem she is having and doesn't seem to know what to do about it, it can be tempting to suggest solutions. Avoid doing this. You can give her the gift of listening to her and accepting her as she is, and you can pray for her later on your own. Likewise, you should avoid asking the group to suggest solutions for situations you are facing. If you feel out of control and need help, ask your group leader to help you find a counselor.

What Materials Are Needed for a Successful Group?

- → Television monitor or screen
- → DVD player
- → Four-session DVD
- → One study guide for each group member (you will be writing in the study guide, so you will each need a copy)
- → Bible(s) (at least one for the group, but encourage all members to bring their Bibles)
- → Pen or pencil for each person

Your Past Has

purpose

Rahab DIDN'T LET HER PAST CONTROL HER FUTURE WITH GOD

We all have a past. And not just any past, a past that is presently living and active—shaping the way we think, believe, and act right this very moment. How we remember our life determines not only the way we relate to ourselves and others, but more importantly, how we relate to God.

For example, some believe their backstory is too boring to be useful: relatively average, safe, no "traumatic" memories to speak of. From this vantage point, God looks more like a frail, old grandpa who would rather "bless our heart" than test us toward a life of suffering and sacrifice in his name. Or perhaps your past feels a bit too scandalous and sinful to be relevant in any plan involving holiness. From this angle, God looks more like a leather-wearing, skin-inked, biker bully than an approachable friend who longs to satisfy your deepest desire.

If you feel unqualified to approach God or be used by him, join the club. The Bible is full of misfits who feel the same way. It is also a book brimming with the unchanging faithfulness of a God who gives meaning and purpose to both boring and scandalous people. In this study we're going to see the truth of this in action through the story of Rahab, a woman in the Bible who didn't let her past control her future with God.

Welcome to the first session of *Rahab: Don't Judge Me, God Says I'm Qualified*. To get started, give everyone a chance to do the following:

→ Say your name, unless everyone in the group knows you. Then, in three or four sentences, describe one of the places where you grew up.

Take a minute on your own to write down your response to this question (you won't have to share your answer):

→ How much do you believe that God can work through you to accomplish his plan for good in the world? A lot? A little? What helps you believe that? What gets in the way?

At a Glance RAHAB

Where in Scripture: Joshua 2

Age-old problem: Being defined by your past and allowing it to determine your future

Rahab's solution: Take a risk, trust God, make a change

God's timeless wisdom: Everything that happens in our life exists to make God more fully known to us and others. From horrific wounding at the hands of an abuser to marrying the love of our life. From a monotonous nine-to-five job to beach sand melting between our toes. Nothing exists for its own sake. Everything exists for the sake of Christ! *"The Son is the image of the invisible God, the firstborn over all creation. For in him all things were created: things in heaven and on earth, visible and invisible, whether thrones or powers or rulers or authorities; all things have been created through him and for him"* (Colossians 1:15–16 NIV).

Play the video segment for Session 1. It's about 23 minutes long, and you will be introduced to three speakers. As you watch, use the following outline to record thoughts that stand out to you.

DRAMA: *Nicole*

Reflecting on the shoes we've worn in our past can remind us of some of the most painful times in our lives.

There are plenty of shoes we never wanted to walk in.

TEACHING: *Jada*

Even if you feel stuck or defined by your old identity, God can re-identify you.

Sometimes you become a part of what your culture says is normal.

We all have religious frames of reference.

To be used on mission, all you have to do is open your heart.

TEACHING: *Kasey*

Sometimes you just need a little pressure to know there's another way.

Pressure points are the catalyst for change.

Somewhere along the way we have created our own version of the truth.

Our truth is designed to help us <u>survive</u>. *God's truth* is designed to help us <u>thrive</u>.

Thriving: Colossians 1:9–14

Rahab knows she needs deliverance, and she is desperate.

Leader, read each numbered prompt to the group.

1 What stood out to you most from the video?

2 What is your honest, gut response to studying Rahab?

3 Our "truth" is a product of the experiences and environment in which we were brought up. What was one experience in your upbringing that made a big impression on you?

4 As a **child** we soak in the way people deal with conflict and love, or not. Share an example from your past.

5 As we move into **adolescence**, we decide if all of these core beliefs are true or false, based on the people around us. Share an example from your past.

6 In our **twenties**, we test-drive those beliefs. Share an example from you past.

7 In our **thirties and forties**, we may realize that there could be another way. Share an example from your past.

8 Think about your upbringing. Describe one way you learned to *give* love (such as cooking meals, giving gifts, spending time, working hard) and one way you were taught to *guard* love (such as expectations, busying yourself, resisting people's demands while avoiding direct confrontation, blame, isolation).

Select a volunteer
to read the following:

God designed us to be shaped by the experiences and environment in which we were brought up. Sadly, we all grow up in a broken world with parents who are broken to a greater or lesser degree. Their challenges affected us profoundly. It would be easy, then, to blame our parents and our society for the difficulties we have. But recognizing where our flaws may have come from doesn't take the sovereignty away from God, nor does it take the responsibility off of us. God wants us to come to grips with the way our past has affected us because he allowed it and intends to use it. We must choose to release our parents and society and learn over time better ways of seeing the world and relating to people. With God's help we can transcend our families and our society and actually contribute to making them better.

9 Is there an identity, name, pair of shoes, or label from your past that you feel stuck with or proud of? If so, what is it? Why does this identity make you feel stuck or proud? Discuss how you might overcome the label or identity.

10 Rahab was desperate for a new way of life. Are there things in your life that you are desperate to change? If so, what are they? Or if you have already made the change, how has your life been affected?

In preparation for the coming week, write one thing you want to gain from your study time:

(ex.: hope for my future, a better understanding of who I am . . .):

Closing Prayer

Ask for a volunteer to read this prayer aloud over the group:

Father God, you know everything about our pasts. Thank you for using all of our regrets, sin, failures, and inadequacies to remind us how desperate we are for a Savior. Thank you for using the best and worst parts, not in spite of us, but because of us. How grateful we are to be women, standing alongside our sister Rahab, qualified to take an active role in your eternal plan and purposes. Strengthen us this week as we open up more, and give us confidence to trust your plan. We pray in Jesus' name, amen.

Keep This Close

As you go on your way this week, here are some thoughts from the video that you may want to save in your phone or write on a sticky note so you can refer back to them:

→ Our truth is designed to help us survive. God's truth is designed to help us thrive.
→ Your past is a part of God's preparation so you can be a significant part of his plan.
→ Even if you feel stuck or defined by your old identity, God has promised to use every part.

On Your Own

Each session of this study also includes activities you can do each day between group meetings. These will help you work through and into a deeper understanding of both the Bible and how it relates to your personal life. **Don't feel you need to do all of these activities. Choose those that are helpful to you. The goal is to grow and develop a stronger relationship with God.** There will be time at the beginning of your next meeting to share whatever you've learned from these activities.

There are many good techniques that may help you memorize Bible verses. Here are some of them:

1. Write out the verse by hand on paper, along with its reference (in this case, Jeremiah 1:5). We remember as much as 80 percent more of what we write by hand than what we type electronically. That's because handwriting stimulates a more helpful part of the brain than typing does.

2. Even better, hand write the verse and reference five times.

3. Read the verse aloud and act it out in an exaggerated way. Proclaim it dramatically. Actors have learned that the dramatic use of your body and voice will create associations in your brain.

4. Go for a walk and recite the verse and reference aloud. Walking increases memory formation.

5. Copy the verse and reference into your phone or onto a card you can keep with you.

6. Return to the verse three times a day to rehearse it. Say it aloud. Do this for all four weeks of this study.

Learning the verse with its reference will help you find it in the Bible if you want to read the larger story around the verse.

Memory Verse

One thing we really hope you'll do is memorize a verse of the Bible. Committing verses to memory enables you to deeply internalize their truth and to have them with you when you need them. Here is the memory verse for Session 1:

> *"Before I formed you in the womb I knew you,*
> *before you were born I set you apart."*
>
> (JEREMIAH 1:5 NIV)

In this verse, God speaks to the young prophet Jeremiah and prepares him for the rough road ahead. He assures him that he, God, set him apart for service long before Jeremiah was aware of it. Everything that had already happened to Jeremiah was preparation for what God had made him for, and everything ahead was going to be woven into God's plan for the good of many people. God speaks these same words to you, because he has also set you apart for his service.

In Real Life:

DRAMA ACTIVITY: Shoes, Part 1

Little, white, patent leather shoes from age five and purple high tops from junior high remind Nicole of some of the most painful times of her life and the shoes she never wanted to walk in.

1 If you were going to tell a story about shoes (or some other artifact) that you didn't want to wear from your childhood, what would the shoes be? What is the story behind those shoes?

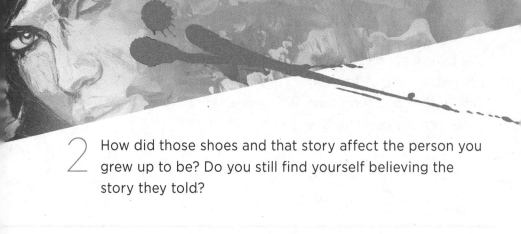

2 How did those shoes and that story affect the person you grew up to be? Do you still find yourself believing the story they told?

3 Have you ever worn shoes simply to "play a part"? If so, describe those shoes and why you wore them.

4 What would it look like to walk in your own shoes?

5   If God were to choose a pair of shoes for you, what do you think they would be like?

The Bible says this about what we wear:

Put on your new nature, and be renewed as you learn to know your Creator and become like him. In this new life, it doesn't matter if you are a Jew or a Gentile, circumcised or uncircumcised, barbaric, uncivilized, slave, or free. Christ is all that matters, and he lives in all of us.

(COLOSSIANS 3:10–11 NLT)

6   What do you think it means to become like your Creator? How do you suppose it's different from becoming like the good church girls you have seen or like whoever else you have tried to live up to?

7   How does it help you to know that it doesn't matter if you are "barbaric, uncivilized, slave, or free" (Colossians

3:11)? The Message translation of this verse may be a bit clearer: "Words like Jewish and non-Jewish, religious and irreligious, insider and outsider, uncivilized and uncouth, slave and free, mean nothing." What other things do you suppose don't matter?

Jesus also says:

Walk with me and work with me—watch how I do it. Learn the unforced rhythms of grace. I won't lay anything heavy or ill-fitting on you. Keep company with me and you'll learn to live freely and lightly."

(MATTHEW 11:29–30 MSG)

What in this passage appeals to you? Why?

9 What is the hard part of doing what Jesus says here?

10 What are you going to do differently in your day-to-day life as a result of this exercise?

Rahab in The Bible

SCRIPTURE ACTIVITY

Look up Joshua 2:1–21 in your Bible and read it.

The Old Testament tells the story of how God chose the family of Abraham to be his means of restoring the whole world to a love relationship with himself. The family became known as the Israelites, and God promised to give them the land of Canaan as their homeland. He told them to drive out the Canaanites, whose culture was riddled with injustices like child sacrifice and ritual prostitution.

The Israelite army's first task was to conquer the walled city of Jericho. The general sent two spies into Jericho to assess the city's defenses. But no matter how well they dressed as Canaanites and spoke the language, their accents would give them away as foreigners. So they went to a house that served as brothel, a likely place for travelers, that happened to be built on top of the extremely wide city wall. This was the house of Rahab.

1 Did Rahab make a deal with the spies before or after she hid them and lied to the king's men? Why is this significant? What does it tell you about her?

(NOTE: Many people dispute whether or not Rahab's lie was justified. Yet this imperfect part of her was still used by God for his plan. When your good intentions fall short of God's perfection, he'll still use you for his purpose.)

2 What reasons does she give for why she hid the spies? What does this tell you about her?

3 How would you describe her faith at this point? For example, what does she believe? Who does she trust, and why? What action is she willing to take to express her faith?

4 How is it significant that Rahab asks the spies to save her extended family, not just her as an individual? What does that say about her?

5 How would you describe Rahab's attitude toward her past in terms of moving forward with her future?

Personal Time Line

TEACHING ACTIVITY

Instructions:

1. Complete a timeline of your life from childhood to age 25 (or to your current age if you're under 25). Note the key people and experiences.

2. Now take some time to write. How did those people and experiences help to shape the person you grew up to be? Use extra paper if necessary.

3. On the timeline, circle any season, choice, or experience that you think disqualifies you from being part of God's people and his mission to the world. Then take some time to pray for God's perspective on your past.

Early Twenties

20
▼

Late Twenties

25
▼

Journal Time

Choose *one* of the following topics to journal about:

→ God met Rahab exactly where she was, using the most broken and messed up parts of her to get her attention. He does the same for you. What are the most broken and messed up parts of you? Maybe they're hidden so nobody sees them. Maybe you don't look at them yourself. But take some time now to look at your past and your present, and the things you do to survive. Write the truth of these things here. Then write about how God has used or is using or can use these things to get your attention.

→ Pressure points tell us things can no longer be the way they have been. What pressure point in your life is pushing you to make a change? What needs to change? How are you responding? What do you think would be the best possible response you could make? What is the hardest part about doing that?

→ Which specific memories from your past tempt you to disbelieve God in your present? Which memories encourage you to believe him more than you have before?

Whichever topic you choose, finish up by writing about this question: What will you do differently in your day-to-day life as a result of this reflection? Again, use extra paper if necessary.

Listening

PRAYER ACTIVITY

God speaks to the heart—the core of you, where your thoughts, emotions, desires, motives, and choices come from. Take some time now to let him speak to you. Find a quiet place where you can be alone. Turn off your phone—or better still, leave it somewhere else so it doesn't draw your eye and your thoughts. Lay before God your thoughts about your past and any doubts you have about whether he can work through you. Then let the busyness of your thoughts go. If you find your mind drifting, just bring it gently back with a calm thought like "Speak, Lord. Your servant is listening."

If you find your mind drifting, easily distracted, or struggle to find downtime in your life, try reading Psalm 139, and listen to what God is saying to you there. God speaks to us in his Spirit. The Spirit is activated through the stimulus of truth. Don't be discouraged if you don't hear an audible message from God. He is always speaking to you through his Holy Word.

Sometimes it helps to read aloud or change up your surroundings. Take a walk, sit on the porch, head to the nearest park bench, or simply sit in your car alone for a few minutes if necessary.

Liking Your reflection

Who do *you* see when you look in the mirror? Do you see a woman who owns her past or feels defeated by it? A woman who welcomes conviction or lingers in condemnation? A victor or a victim?

If we are honest, most of us see some of both depending on the day. Rahab would live victoriously in God, but like all of us who are brave enough to look in the mirror, she would first need to reflect on the very real wounding she experienced over the course of her life. We all have wounding.

In Rahab's case, she was a prostitute, using her body to survive, treating love as something to be bought and sold. She had years of patterns built up to protect her heart from hurt. We may never have been literal prostitutes, yet we all have patterns of thought and behavior that we created to survive but that block us from giving and receiving love as we were designed to do.

In this session we'll consider what can happen when we start letting go of those habits of self-protection and unforgiveness.

Check In

Before you dive into the video, take a few minutes to check in with each other. Let each person choose one of the following questions to respond to:

→ What did you get out of the "On Your Own" exercises you did for Session 1?

→ How were you or weren't you shown love as a child? Please keep your answer under two minutes.

Next, say your memory verse aloud together. Be sure to say the verse reference after it. If you don't know the verse from memory yet, read it with the group from page 25.

At a Glance: RAHAB

Age-old problem: Being hurt by others

Age-old mistake: Building walls of self-protection

God's timeless wisdom: As we are increasingly secure in God's love, we will increasingly tear down the walls of self-protection. *"And may you have the power to understand, as all God's people should, how wide, how long, how high, and how deep his love is. May you experience the love of Christ, though it is too great to understand fully. Then you will be made complete with all the fullness of life and power that comes from God"* (Ephesians 3:18–19 NLT).

Play the video segment for Session 2. It's about 18 minutes long. As you watch, use the following outline to record thoughts that stand out to you.

DRAMA: Nicole

We can easily begin to keep score with or rate other people. God does not keep score.

TEACHING: Kasey

Love as a commodity.

The more hurt we are, the deeper debts go, blocking the free flow of love.

There is no room for unconditional love in our life when we're hanging onto debts.

Colossians 2:13-14

The love that God offers us is a love without condition, a love that requires nothing from us.

Leader, read each numbered prompt to the group.

1 What stood out to you most from the video?

2 Kasey said, "All I had learned throughout my childhood, my teen years, and my twenties was that love was something that could be earned, that there was a price tag on it, that it was a commodity. I learned to exchange it, to give it only when I got something in return, and to return it only when someone needed nothing from me."

Can you identify with treating love as a commodity to be earned and traded for other things you want? Or have you learned to give and receive unconditional love? Describe how you deal with love.

3 What kinds of things do people trade for love?

4 How do we use our femininity to get what we want? Give some examples.

5 Think about Rahab's situation as a prostitute in her culture. Why do you think she had to wall off her emotions and eradicate her need for love in order to survive?

6 One of the things we do when we have been hurt and haven't forgiven is come up with strategies to protect ourselves from being hurt again. One strategy Kasey named is keeping emotional distance from others, not letting them get close to our honest, vulnerable parts. How might we go about keeping emotional distance from others? What behaviors might that involve?

7 What are some of the unintended consequences of keeping others at a distance?

8 Given that not forgiving others causes us problems, it might seem that the simple solution is to forgive them. But forgiveness is often hard. What do you think holds us back from letting others off the hook for what we feel they owe us?

Select a volunteer
to read the following:

We see ourselves as vulnerable and in need of protection. We also believe that it's up to us to protect ourselves, or possibly to get somebody else to protect us. So we read with incomprehension the words and actions of Jesus, such as these:

> "But I say to you who hear, Love your enemies, do good to those who hate you, bless those who curse you, pray for those who abuse you. To one who strikes you on the cheek, offer the other also, and from one who takes away your cloak do not withhold your tunic either. Give to everyone who begs from you, and from one who takes away your goods do not demand them back. . . . If you love those who love you, what benefit is that to you? For even sinners love those who love them." (Luke 6:27–30, 32 ESV)

Jesus thinks it's up to God to protect us. He knows God won't protect us from all hurt, but he views hurt as not disastrous because he knows God will be with us in our hurt. Hurt can't destroy us as long as we're reliant on God. This is what helps him forgive quickly and cleanly, and to extend love to those who hurt him.

9 Colossians 2:13-14 says that God has canceled the debt we owe to him. Does that make it easier for you to cancel the debts that others owe you? Why or why not?

10 God loves us without needing anything from us and without our having to return his love adequately. Have you experienced that love? If so, give an example of how you have experienced it. If not, how do you respond to the idea of it?

In preparation for the coming week, write one thing you want to gain from your study time:

(ex.: hope for my future, a better understanding of who I am ...):

Closing Prayer

Ask for a volunteer to read this prayer aloud over the group:

Jesus, you know all the things we have done to others that make us feel that we owe them. You know all that others have done to us that make us feel that they owe us. And you know the many ways we have built up debt against you by not loving and honoring you as you deserve and by not treating the people you created as you wanted them to be treated. Yet you came to earth to pay for our debts against you. If we accept that generosity, we owe you nothing but gratitude. Please help each one of us experience your unconditional love and be changed by it. Please help us forgive and let go of our grip on our strategies of self-protection. We want to be able to love. We pray in your name, amen.

Keep This Close

As you go on your way this week, here are some thoughts from the video that you may want to save in your phone or write on a sticky note so you can refer back to them:

→ The extent of our self-protection is directly correlated to the amount of unforgiveness or resentment built up in our hearts.
→ Self-protection has unintended consequences that block us from giving and receiving love.

On Your Own

Memory Verse

This week, continue to practice saying aloud your memory verse:

"Before I formed you in the womb I knew you, before you were born I set you apart."

(JEREMIAH 1:5 NIV)

In Real Life:

DRAMA ACTIVITY: Keeping Score

Nicole plays Susan, the daughter of an investment banker. Growing up, Susan got affection from her father when the market was up but withdrawal when the market was down. Susan learned to feel that she was a stock whose value went up or down depending on what she did. She began keeping score on herself in a journal, and eventually she started keeping score on other people. Finally, a friend accidentally picked up and read part of her journal and challenged her thinking about it.

1 Do you keep score on yourself? If so, what gives you a higher score?

What gives you a lower score?

Where does your rating system come from?

How does keeping score affect what you do?

2 Do you keep score on other people? If so, what gives
   them a higher or lower score?

How does keeping score affect the way you relate to them?

3 How many times this week have you lied on Facebook
   or purposely posted on Instagram just chasing the
   fulfillment of what others might think?

When you do that, how do you end up feeling?

How is your social media presentation of yourself different
from the whole story about you?

4   Do you think other people lie on social media to impress
    readers? How does that affect the way you think about,
    feel about, and respond to their posts?

5   If you were going to create the most honest Twitter
    profile ever, what would you say?

6   Susan's friend says God doesn't keep score. Do you
    believe that deep down? What persuades you to believe it
    or not believe it?

7   The best way to know whether God keeps score is to sit
    down and read through an account of Jesus' ministry
    and see how he operated. You might start with Luke
    chapter 4 and read through to the end of the book. If you
    don't have time for that right now, here are some shorter
    passages, some printed out for you and others that you
    can look up. What does each of them say related to the
    topic of whether God keeps score?

    Matthew 18:21–22

[Love] keeps no record of being wronged. (1 Corinthians 13:5 NLT)

Salvation is not a reward for the good things we have done, so none of us can boast about it. (Ephesians 2:9 NLT)

Luke 7:36–50

YOU can know that you have some **DEBT TO DEAL WITH** in your life anywhere you are **WATERING DOWN** your story, anywhere you are **HIDING OUT** from the things that have really *happened to you*

TEACHING ACTIVITY

Kasey said, "You can know that you have some debt to deal with in your life anywhere you are watering down your story, anywhere you are hiding out from the things that have really happened to you."

What parts of your story do you water down or exaggerate? In what specific groups of people do you most often do this?

Sometimes hiding out goes beyond watering something down. It can mean not telling anyone about it at all. You know you're doing this if you have never told anyone the story. You especially know if you have been lying to yourself about the story, saying it never happened, changing what really happened to something better, or putting up walls to avoid thinking about it. If you tell yourself, "That's in the past; I don't go there," you are hiding out. Chances are high that it is still affecting who you are in the present, what you choose to do and not do, how close you let people come. It may be fueling coping strategies that numb your feelings, strategies like staying constantly busy, compulsively checking your phone, living on social media, binge eating, or shopping with money you can't really afford.

What is that story you are hiding from? What is that moment, that experience, those events, that hurt? Is there anybody in your life you can imagine telling the story to? If not, consider making an appointment with a professional counselor.

Or, begin by writing about the story. Write as much as you can about what happened. You can write it somewhere other than this book if you want to keep it secure. Writing can help you untangle the story you have been telling yourself from the story of what really happened. It can help you understand bits that haven't made sense. You may see that what happened wasn't your fault. You can set boundaries around the writing, like telling yourself you only have to write for ten minutes and then you can stop and do something good for yourself.

Don't want to write about it? Make a drawing. Draw some detail that sticks in your mind, like the orange bedspread. Or draw the room. Or draw an abstract picture of the feeling that goes with the experience.

Rahab in the Bible

SCRIPTURE ACTIVITY

Look up Joshua 6:1-25 and read it.

1 What do you think might have been going through Rahab's mind as the events of verses 8-14 took place? Remember that she didn't know what God had told Joshua.

2 What might Rahab have learned about God from watching the city walls collapse without the Israelites attacking them?

3 In verses 22-23, Rahab and her family were rescued. How might that have affected her relationship with God? What might she have believed about God then?

4   For the rest of her life, Rahab knew she was noticed by God. What she had witnessed could have left her hopeless, but it didn't. She knew that she would have a different experience of life going forward, and that God was for her and not against her. How do you think knowing those things would affect the way a person feels and acts in life?

5   Do you know you are noticed by God? Do you know he is for you, not against you? How do you want your life to be affected by knowing that?

Journal Time

Choose *one* of the following topics to journal about:

→ What is the difference between unconditional and conditional love? What experience have you had of unconditional love, if any? How has it affected the way you feel, the way you think, the way you act? Or if you can't remember ever experiencing unconditional love, how has that affected you?

→ Are you secretly holding out for an apology or acknowledgment of offense from someone? If so, how do you think receiving this would help you? How have you been living with this offense without an apology since it happened? What would it cost you to forgive this person, to cancel their debt? What is not forgiving them costing you?

→ Do you find yourself sabotaging relationships the closer they get? If so, what scares you most about the commitment and vulnerability required for godly friendship? Where do you think that fear comes from?

Whichever topic(s) you choose, finish up by writing about this question: What will you do differently in your day-to-day life as a result of this reflection? Again, use extra paper if needed.

PRAYER ACTIVITY

Have a dialogue with God about love. Tell him what you have been settling for apart from him, and ask him for whole, eternal, and unconditional love. Ask for the kind of love that cancels your debts and leaves you with a clean slate. Open yourself to receive it. Talk with him about what it's like for you to do that. If you're afraid of him for any reason, tell him about that, and ask him to help you entrust your fear to him.

What's in a reputation?

Rahab had a complicated past. Really complicated. She carried wounds that affected how well she was able to give and receive love. But the downsides of her life were far from the whole story with her. God had made her with some unique qualities that equipped her to act effectively for him when the Israelite spies came to her door. He knew her long before this incident, and he had shaped her from before birth to be the woman he had planned for her to be. When he looked at her, he saw her wounds, but he also saw her strengths. These were qualities she was going to carry forward into her new life as his follower, and they would equip her to continue to serve him effectively.

In this study you're going to reflect on your own God-given personality and consider what strengths you have that equip you to serve him. Some of us have a much easier time seeing our deficits than our strengths, and that's where your group comes in: even if they have known you for only a couple of weeks, they may already be able to see some of the things about you that you can't see. God has purposes and goals for your life. The more you seek him, the more you'll become aware of what those are.

Check In

Before you dive into the video, take a few minutes to check in with each other. Give everyone a chance to respond to the following questions:

→ What did you get out of the "On Your Own" practices you did for Session 2?
→ What is one positive personality trait you have?

Next, say your memory verse aloud together. Be sure to say the verse reference with it.

At a Glance RAHAB

Age-old problem: Having a complicated personality

Age-old mistake: Feeling like we don't fit in

God's timeless wisdom: God made us the way we are, and he will use us with the personality we have. *"Your eyes saw my unformed body; all the days ordained for me were written in your book before one of them came to be"* (Psalm 139:16 NIV).

Play the video segment for Session 3. It's about 20 minutes long. As you watch, use the following outline to record thoughts that stand out to you.

DRAMA: Nicole

What would Rahab have tweeted?

TEACHING: Jada

Rahab was bold and smart and strategic.

Whoever you are today is who God is going to use.

Joshua 2:9-11
> When you observe the greatness of God, you melt, you submit.

The Proverbs 31 woman.

Psalm 139:13

Be the best version of yourself.

Whoever you are today is who GOD is going to use.

Leader, read each numbered prompt to the group.

1 What stood out to you most from the video?

2 How did Jada's description of Rahab's personality fit with a person who (according to Kasey in Session 2) had been hurt and was treating love as a commodity? Is it possible to be both?

3 If Rahab had had a Twitter account, what else do you think she would have tweeted?

4 How does it affect you to think of Rahab having qualities of the Proverbs 31 woman?

Select a volunteer
to read the following:

One reason it helps to think of Rahab as a Proverbs 31 woman is that it dispels myths about that chapter of the Bible. For example, the chapter isn't a checklist that we are expected to live up to completely. It portrays an ideal woman, and even brand-new believer Rahab was living up to some of her qualities. Rahab wasn't married. She didn't have children. She had a couple of jobs and was supporting a family. She was damaged in some significant ways. And she had a lot to offer. We need to avoid looking at Proverbs 31 as a checklist of how we fall short of God's expectations. He made us the way we are, even if we never get up "while it is still night" (Proverbs 31:15).

5 How would you describe your personality? How do you think God sees you? If it's hard for you to come up with words that describe you, you can scan the list of words under "Journal Time" on page 78

6 How are you like Rahab? How are you different?

7 How can God use someone like you for his purposes?

8 What aspects of your personality and character do you think God wants to change? What aspects do you think he wants to keep as they are?

9 How easy is it for you to celebrate the way God made you? Why is that the case?

10 Rahab had the label "prostitute." But she didn't let it keep her from taking effective action or from moving toward God. Do you have a label or reputation that has been holding you back from embracing the way God sees you? If so, how can you begin to move past it and into who God says you are?

11 Rahab's heart melted when she heard about the greatness of God (Joshua 2:9–11). What has made your heart melt? How has that affected your choices?

In preparation for the coming week, write one thing you want to gain from your study time:

(ex.: hope for my future, a better understanding of who I am . . .):

Closing Prayer

Ask for a volunteer to read this prayer aloud over the group:

God, you made each one of us with our unique personality. Please help us to see and value the strengths you have given us. Show us how we can use them to do things in the world that you have purposed in us from before time began. We are grateful that even though you don't need us, you want us—that you desire to partner with us in accomplishing good things in the world. Please bring good even out of the aspects of ourselves that we perceive as weaknesses, revealing your strength in our weakness. Speak humility into our heart and melt any part of our personality we are clinging to more than you. Convict us—help us change. May we be women who see and affirm what is valuable in one another; celebrating instead of comparing, encouraging instead of criticizing. We ask these things in Jesus' name, amen.

Keep This Close

As you go on your way this week, here are some thoughts from the video that you may want to save in your phone or write on a sticky note so you can refer back to them:

→ Whoever you are today is who God is going to use.
→ When you observe, even indirectly, the greatness of God, your heart has but one response: to melt, to bow down, to submit yourself to the one true living God.
→ Don't spend your time trying to be some sad version of someone else when all you need to do is be the best version of yourself.

On Your Own

Memory Verse

This week, continue to practice saying
aloud your memory verse:

*"Before I formed you in the womb I knew you,
before you were born I set you apart."*

(Jeremiah 1:5 NIV)

In Real Life:

DRAMA ACTIVITY: Tweets

1 Nicole speculated on some of the tweets Rahab might have
had if she'd had a Twitter account. You had a little time in
the group meeting to share your ideas for tweets, but now
think a little deeper. Look again at Joshua 2 if it's helpful.
What might have been some of Rahab's tweets or posts . . .

→ Before the spies came to Jericho, when the rumors
about the Israelites were flying around town?

→ After the spies left her house, during the weeks when
she was waiting for the Israelites to return?

→ After the Israelites destroyed Jericho, and she was
getting used to her new life?

2 What might she tweet or post if she observed life in your world today? Think about how her personality would react to your life and the world you live in.

3 What kind of a person are you on social media? How are you like or unlike the way you are in real life? If you're not sure, go back and read some old posts as if they were posted by someone else. What kind of person do you see?

4 What kind of a person would you like to be on social media? Why?

5 Read Colossians 3:12–15. What is hard about living this way on social media? Write down the qualities that are especially hard.

Why do you suppose these qualities are so hard to practice on social media?

6 Verse 12 says one thing that helps us develop these qualities is reminding ourselves that we are God's chosen ones, holy, and beloved. Do you think of yourself as chosen? What about as beloved? What helps you or gets in the way?

7 How do you think taking on this way of viewing yourself as part of your identity could help you on social media?

8 What are you going to do differently in your day-to-day life as a result of this exercise?

SCRIPTURE ACTIVITY

Look up Matthew 1:1–6 and read it.

Rahab is mentioned three times in the New Testament. The first time is right at the beginning, in the first chapter of Matthew, a genealogy of Jesus that lots of readers skip over.

1   This genealogy (which continues through verse 16) mainly mentions Jesus' male ancestors, but these opening verses mention four of the women who were his foremothers. Does it surprise you that Rahab is highlighted in Jesus' family line (verse 5), even though she was a prostitute and a non-Israelite? What does this say about the message of this genealogy?

2   The other three women mentioned in these verses are:

→ Tamar (verse 3). She was Judah's daughter-in-law, but her husband and Judah's second son died. By law Judah should have married her to his third son so she could have children in her late husband's family line, but Judah was afraid she was a curse on the family, so he let her languish. To get her rights, Tamar disguised herself as a prostitute and seduced Judah. When she became pregnant, she produced proof that she wasn't just sleeping around and that Judah was the father. Thus she secured her place in the family (Genesis 38). This is how Perez was born and got into Jesus' family line.

→ Ruth (verse 5). She was an impeccably virtuous woman but from a hated foreign country, Moab. The law said, *"No Ammonite or Moabite or any of their descendants may enter the assembly of the Lord, not even in the tenth generation" (Deuteronomy 23:3 NIV).* Yet a good Israelite named Boaz married her, and she was welcomed into his clan, and her great-grandson David was anointed as king of Israel.

→ Bathsheba ("Uriah's wife," verse 6). Matthew makes a point of saying that before she was King David's wife, she was Uriah's wife. David seduced her, and then when she got pregnant he had Uriah murdered so he could marry her (2 Samuel 11).

Why do you think Matthew included the names of these women in Jesus' genealogy? What do you think he was trying to say by including them?

3 How does it affect you to think of Jesus with these women highlighted in his family line?

Hebrews 11 gives a long catalog of Old Testament people who lived by faith. The list is intended to encourage readers to live by faith too. Read the following excerpts from this chapter:

> ¹ Now faith is confidence in what we hope for and assurance about what we do not see. ² This is what the ancients were commended for. . . .
>
> ⁶ And without faith it is impossible to please God, because anyone who comes to him must believe that he exists and that he rewards those who earnestly seek him. . . .
>
> ³¹ By faith the prostitute Rahab, because she welcomed the spies, was not killed with those who were disobedient. . . .
>
> ³⁹ These were all commended for their faith, yet none of them received what had been promised, ⁴⁰ since God had planned something better for us so that only together with us would they be made perfect. (Hebrews 11:1–2, 6, 31, 39–40 NIV)

4 The writer defines the word *faith* in verse 1. How did Rahab show confidence in what she hoped for? What did she hope for? (You can look back at Joshua 2).

How did she show assurance in what she didn't see?

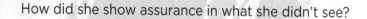

5 How is this kind of faith different from simply believing a set of facts about God?

How is it different from self-confidence, or confidence in the universe?

6 Verse 6 says "without faith it is impossible to please God." Why is that the case?

What are the implications of this fact for us?

7 Verses 39-40 say that Rahab (and the other people listed in the chapter) didn't receive what God had promised. That was because she and the others were waiting for something more than they ever experienced in their lifetimes, something God fulfilled only with the coming of Jesus. How do you respond to the idea of remaining faithful for your whole life, waiting for something that won't be fulfilled until after you're dead? Can you have faith like that? Why or why not?

8 What is your personal takeaway from these passages from Matthew and Hebrews?

Journal Time

Below are a series of words that describe positive or neutral personality traits. Circle *three to five* of these that you think are true of you. Then journal about these, describing how they play out in your life and how they equip you to contribute to good in the world.

inventive	curious	consistent
love art	passionate	adventurous
cooperative	imaginative	systematic
love reading	practical	good with data
energetic	assertive	perceptive
self-disciplined	good planner	spontaneous
sociable	reflective	outgoing
compassionate	good with computers	friendly
helpful	well-tempered	trustworthy
not easily fooled	confident	secure
stable	dynamic	adaptable
reasonable	enthusiastic	communicative
bold	expressive	sympathetic
warm	tactful	firm
thorough	industrious	tireless
versatile	diplomatic	deep
cautious	independent	intellectual
flexible	thoughtful	organized
analytical	moderate	persistent
kind	dependable	patient

PRAYER ACTIVITY

Write a letter to God telling him *one* of the following:

→ The things about your personality and character that make you unsure whether you fit in with God's people or have the potential to serve God powerfully.

→ The things about your personality and character that people in your childhood or adulthood made fun of or said were negatives.

List the things here to reference in your letter.

Now write God's response. If you like, write out Romans 8:31–39 or Ephesians 2:1–10.

You Have
a choice

As women, many of us spend a lot of time listing all the reasons why we're not qualified. We're not good at something. There's something wrong with us. We can't succeed. We're damaged goods. We'll fail, so why try? But through the life of Rahab, we see the only bullet point that matters: *In Christ, we are qualified.* Through his death, we can kill off every lie on that list. Through his resurrection, we can give life to new thoughts and behaviors. Rahab was a damaged prostitute. She was considered an unimportant person where she came from. She was raised in a corrupt, anti-God culture—a culture so bad that God intended to wipe it off the map. Yet none of that disqualified her from doing something great for God's plan. She didn't let the fear of failure stop her from trying. She didn't let the judgment her culture deserved stop her from reaching out and asking for deliverance from that judgment. She went from judged to qualified because of one thing: choosing to believe in the real God and who he said she was.

In this final session, we'll see that this God knows exactly what it's like to be us because he has walked this earth in our shoes. We'll see that he covers our shame and protects our vulnerable parts. And we'll see that he has made us fully qualified to participate in what he is doing in the world. We have everything we need. All we need to do is trust and respond.

Check In

Before you dive into the video, take a few minutes to check in with each other. Let each person choose one of the following to respond to:

→ What did you get out of the "On Your Own" practices you did for Session 3?

→ Where did you see God at work in your life this week? Or where did you hope to see him and didn't?

Next, say your memory verse aloud together, along with its reference.

At a Glance RAHAB

Age-old problem: Having flaws and weaknesses

Age-old mistake: Disqualifying ourselves from God's service

God's timeless wisdom: God makes us qualified. He uses everything we have been for his mission. *"For we are God's masterpiece. He has created us anew in Christ Jesus, so we can do the good things he planned for us long ago" (Ephesians 2:10 NLT).*

Play the video segment for Session 4. It's about 20 minutes long. As you watch, use the following outline to record thoughts that stand out to you.

DRAMA: *Nicole*

Jesus didn't come to save us from our circumstances. He came to find us in the midst of them, so that we could know he knows right where we're walking.

When God knocks, we open the door and the journey, as hard as it is, will never be wasted.

TEACHING: *Jada*

One of the most dangerous things women do to themselves is disqualification.

Everyone has had opportunities to respond to God.

Is your background or personality diminishing your hope?

Even if things don't change overnight, we can trust God that he is working them out. Hope is going to come to fruition.

TEACHING: *Kasey*

Before Rahab was in the womb, God knew her and formed her for purpose and meaning.

The curse on Noah's son Ham: Genesis 9:18–27.

Prophecy is a message that aligns with the already finished will of God.

Hesed (kindness in Joshua 2:12–14) means a love that covers, protects, keeps safe.

God does not point out our shame, vulnerabilities, weaknesses. Instead, he covers them.

God is going to restore all that has been exposed, all that has been violated.

Leader, read each numbered prompt to the group.

1 What stood out to you most from the video?

2 How does it affect you to think of God having walked in your shoes and wasting nothing you have been through?

3 Jada said, "I think that one of the most dangerous things that women do to themselves is disqualification." What does it mean to disqualify yourself? How do we as women do it?

How is disqualification a choice?

4 Rahab had *"the assurance of things hoped for"* (Hebrews 11:1 ESV). What do you hope for? How much assurance do you have that you will one day get it?

Select a volunteer
to read the following:

Hope is longing for something you don't yet have. The more you want it, the more you ache. *"Hope deferred makes the heart sick"* (Proverbs 13:12). Because many of us have had our hopes disappointed and betrayed way too often, we have tried to deaden the ache of hope in our hearts. But deadening hope also deadens other things in our hearts, like the capacity for joy and generous love. We become tough. Things don't get to us. And people don't get through to the real us either. When that happens, coming back alive to hope and love takes time and commitment. We have to be willing to feel the sadness of our losses and disappointments. And we need a vision of what God offers us that we can hope for with confidence. We have a choice to make.

5 How do we know if we are hoping for the right things?

6 Could your past or your personality be diminishing your hope? If so, how?

Select a volunteer
to read the following:

In Joshua 2:12–14, Rahab and the men use the Hebrew word *hesed*. It is often translated as "loving-kindness" or "covenant love" or "kindness." Here is the passage with the words translating *hesed* in italics:

> "Now then, please swear to me by the Lord that, as I have dealt *kindly* with you, you also will deal kindly with my father's house, and give me a sure sign that you will save alive my father and mother, my brothers and sisters, and all who belong to them, and deliver our lives from death." And the men said to her, "Our life for yours even to death! If you do not tell this business of ours, then when the Lord gives us the land we will deal *kindly* and faithfully with you." (Joshua 2:12–14 ESV)

Hesed means a love that covers, that protects, that keeps safe.

7   Why did Rahab need a love that covers, protects, and keeps safe?

Why do we need that same kind of love?

8   Why is it important that God doesn't point out our shame but instead covers it? How can that affect the way we feel and live?

9   When you think of God restoring all that has been exposed and violated, what do you think that will look like and feel like?

10 You answered the following question at the beginning of Session 1 (pg. 14). Take a minute on your own and write down how you would respond to it now: How much do you believe that God can work through you to accomplish his plan for good in the world? A lot? A little? What helps you believe that? What gets in the way?

11 Discuss this with your group: What are you grateful for that you've received from this study on Rahab? What will you take with you?

In preparation for the coming week, write one thing you want to gain from your study time:

(*ex.: hope for my future, a better understanding of who I am . . .*):

Closing Prayer

Ask for a volunteer to read this prayer aloud over the group:

God, thank you for your love that covers our vulnerabilities and shame, that protects, that keeps safe. Thank you for revealing yourself to us and inviting us to respond to you. Thank you for walking in our shoes and knowing, really knowing, what it is like to be us. Please help us not to disqualify ourselves, but instead, actively engage our story—looking for ways to renew our past, not run from it. Please help us to respond to you with hope, with faith, like Rahab. We give to you all of our doubts that you can work through us to accomplish your good plan, and we trust that you can use us with all of our complicated history and personality. Please show us our next step. We pray in Jesus' name, amen.

Keep This Close

As you go on your way this week, here are some thoughts from the video that you may want to save in your phone or write on a sticky note so you can refer back to them:

→ I don't have to be stuck. I can be used by the sovereign God.
→ God is going to restore all that has been exposed, all that has been violated.

On Your Own

Memory Verse

Continue to practice saying aloud your
memory verse:

*"Before I formed you in the womb I knew you,
before you were born I set you apart."*

(JEREMIAH 1:5 NIV)

In Real Life:

DRAMA ACTIVITY: Shoes, Part 2

Nicole took us back to the story of the shoes she wore as a child and teen, and she realized that God had gone to find her right in the middle of agonizing circumstances. He has wasted nothing she has been through.

1   How well do the shoes that Jesus has given you fit your feet? Do you still need Band-Aids or cushions? Why?

2   What does walking in the shoes designed just for you feel like?

3 Do you still want to wear someone else's shoes, or are you able to value your own? Describe what you value about yours or whose shoes you would rather wear.

4 When Peter had doubts about whether non-Jews could become fully qualified followers of Jesus, God gave him a vision. In the vision God said, *"Do not call something unclean if God has made it clean" (Acts 11:9 NLT).* How do these words apply to you today?

5 Paul worked for the arrest and murder of Christians before he had a vision of Jesus and changed his views. He then went on to use everything he had learned as a Jewish student and all of his experience as a forgiven man with blood on his hands to form the message he shared with people about Jesus. Read 1 Timothy 1:12–17 Can you identify with Paul calling himself the foremost sinner (verse 15), or does that seem foreign to you? Why?

According to Paul, why did he receive mercy (verse 16)?

Does this help to explain to you why you have received mercy? Explain.

6 Read Psalm 139:14. Can you authentically say, "I am wonderfully made"? What helps you? What gets in the way?

SCRIPTURE ACTIVITY

Read James 2:14–26.

In Hebrews 11, the writer points to Rahab as an example of faith. James, the brother of Jesus, also writes about Rahab and faith. They both agree that faith isn't simply agreeing with information about God. Rahab chose to believe she was worth God noticing her—she was qualified to be loved because He said she was. And then she acted on that conviction.

1 What is the true connection between conviction and action (verse 22)?

2 How did Rahab express her conviction in action (verse 25)?

3 Do you believe you are qualified to be loved because
   God says you are? As this study draws to a close, what
   encourages you to believe this? Does anything still get in
   the way?

4 How could you express in action your conviction about
   being qualified?

5 What is your personal takeaway from thinking about the
   connection between conviction and action? How would
   you say it if you were going to post it online?

Journal Time

Choose *one* of the following topics to reflect on:

→ Romans 1:20 means that everybody has had opportunities to respond to God. What opportunities have you had? How have you responded to those opportunities? Which ones have you made excuses about or disqualified yourself for? Which ones have you responded to with faith and action? What do you want to do now?

→ Do you have a habit of disqualifying yourself? If so, how does that tend to play out? Where do you think the habit comes from?

→ Think about God restoring all that has been exposed and violated in you. Let yourself imagine that this is in the process of happening. How will you be different? How will that change the choices that have become automatic in you?

→ *Hesed* is a love that covers, protects, and keeps safe. Why do you need that kind of love? How will it affect your life if you get it?

Whichever topic you choose, finish up by writing about this question: What will you do differently in your day-to-day life as a result of THIS STUDY?

Take Action

What would it look like for you to put faith like Rahab's into action? To what deeds is God calling you? Spend some time in prayer about this. Look around you at the needs of people in your world. Consider your personality, your skills, and your other resources. In *Wishful Thinking*, the writer Frederick Buechner says, "The place God calls you to is the place where your deep gladness and the world's deep hunger meet." Write down your thoughts about steps you can take to contribute to what God is doing in the world.

About the Authors

Jada Edwards, Bible Teacher, Speaker, Author

Jada is an experienced Bible teacher and has committed her life to equipping women of all ages with practical, biblical truth. She currently serves as the Women's Pastor and as the Director of Creative Services for One Community Church in Plano, Texas. Jada teaches a midweek women's Bible study to over 1,300 women each week. She has authored two books based on her Bible studies: *Captive Mind* and *Thirst*. She and her husband, Conway, have a son, Joah, and a daughter, Chloe.

Nicole Johnson, Dramatist and Author

A bestselling author, performer, and motivational speaker, Nicole is one of the most sought-after creative communicators in America today. Her unique ability to blend humor with compassion, as she captures the inner-most feelings of women facing life's daily struggles, has enabled her to create a unique sense of community for women of all ages. Nicole has 20 years' experience as an actor, television host, and producer, and has published eight books and a variety of curricula regarding relationships. She has written and performed sketches for the Women of Faith Conferences and written and directed dramas for The Revolve Tour. For three years, she wrote and performed dramatic sketches with relationship expert Dr. Gary Smalley, bringing her unique perspective to his seminars.

Kasey Van Norman, Author, Bible Teacher, Counselor

Kasey is a bestselling author, licensed counselor, and Bible teacher living in Bryan, Texas with her husband, Justin, and their two children, Emma Grace and Lake. Kasey has published two books and two Bible studies, *Named by God* and *Raw Faith*. Kasey teaches and writes about the love that redeemed her life from the shame of past abuse, addiction, infidelity, and the fear of a life-threatening cancer diagnosis. She teaches thousands of women each year as a ministry event speaker—a headliner with the Extraordinary Women Conferences and American Association of Christian Counselors, and as an ambassador with Compassion International.

KNOWN
BY
Name

The women in the Bible asked the same three questions we all still ask today:

How does everyone else see me?

How do I see myself?

How does God see me?

The Known by Name series explores complex women in the Bible and their struggles with tough questions through the lenses of a counselor, a Bible teacher, and a dramatist.

Kasey Van Norman is a bestselling author, licensed counselor, and Bible teacher living in Texas with her husband and their two children. Kasey teaches and writes about the love that redeemed her life from the shame of past abuse, addiction, infidelity, and the fear of a life-threatening cancer diagnosis.

Jada Edwards is an experienced Bible teacher committed to equipping women of all ages with practical, biblical truth. She currently serves as the Women's Pastor and Director of Creative Services for One Community Church in Plano, Texas. She and her husband have two children.

Nicole Johnson, bestselling author, performer, and motivational speaker, is one of the most sought-after creative communicators in America today. She uniquely blends humor with compassion, creating a sense of community for women of all ages. She makes California home with her husband and children.

RAHAB

Don't Judge Me,
God Says I'm

Qualified

HAGAR

In the Face of Rejection,
God Says I'm

Significant

NAOMI

When I Feel Worthless,
God Says I'm

Enough

Rahab's story, found in the book of Joshua, is a story of a girl boss, an assertive, confident woman who did what she had to do to provide for her family. Her identity was shaped by her upbringing. With no Bible study to join or podcast to download, Rahab learned her behaviors in a culture that believed in gods, not God. But when opportunity knocked, she boldly trusted in God, and became a woman who brought freedom to generations.

This four-session video Bible study will take you through the story of Rahab, our sister in Scripture who trusted God's final word about her worth above society's. Through her story, you will learn how to shed unhelpful labels and fears, and instead revel in God's unconditional love and acceptance of you—just as you are.

Hagar's story, found in Genesis 16, is a story of cultural victimization. She was betrayed, abandoned, and scorned. Her response? She did what most of us would do when deeply hurt by someone we trust—she ran away. She got defensive. She retreated to a place where she felt safe. She felt justified in her anger and hurt. But deep in her core was a woman who longed to be seen and hoped for redemption.

This four-session video Bible study will take you through the story of Hagar, our sister in Scripture who learns through hurt and rejection that what is unresolved is not unseen by God. Through her story, you will learn how to respond when life doesn't affirm you, but God does.

Naomi's story, found in the book of Ruth, is a story of lost identity. She lost her husband and her sons, which in her culture left her completely without a home or a means to support herself. She was a Hebrew woman in Moabite territory, alone among strangers. She reacted by letting her circumstances define her. But even in her angry, fearful, rather dramatic season of feeling like the victim, God kept showing his faithfulness.

This four-session video Bible study will take you through the story of Naomi, our sister in Scripture who traveled from comfort and security to despair and bitterness; from hopeless drifting to faithful obedience; from loss to redemption in one short lifetime.

Available now at your favorite bookstore.

BIBLE STUDY
SOURCE
for women

powered by ChurchSource

Connecting you with the best in

BIBLE STUDY RESOURCES

from many of the world's

MOST TRUSTED BIBLE TEACHERS

SHAUNA NIEQUIST   **MARGARET FEINBERG**   **ANN VOSKAMP**   **CHRISTINE CAINE**

Providing
WOMEN'S MINISTRY LEADERS,
SMALL GROUP LEADERS, AND INDIVIDUALS

with the
INSPIRATION, ENCOURAGEMENT, AND RESOURCES
every woman needs to grow their faith in every season of life

powered by ChurchSource

join our
COMMUNITY

Use our BIBLE STUDY FINDER to quickly find the perfect study for your group, learn more about all the new studies available, and download FREE printables to help you make the most of your Bible study experience.

BibleStudySourceForWomen.com

FIND THE *perfect* BIBLE STUDY
for you and your group in 5 MINUTES or LESS!

*Find the right study for your women's group
by answering four easy questions:*

1. WHAT TYPE OF STUDY DO YOU WANT TO DO?

- *Book of the Bible:* Dive deep into the study of a Bible character, or go through a complete book of the Bible systematically, or add tools to your Bible study methods toolkit.
- *Topical Issues:* Have a need in a specific area of life? Study the Scriptures that pertain to that need. Topics include prayer, joy, purpose, balance, identity in Christ, and more.

2. WHAT LEVEL OF TIME COMMITMENT BETWEEN SESSIONS WOULD YOU LIKE?

- *None:* No personal homework
- *Minimal:* Less than 30 minutes of homework
- *Moderate:* 30 minutes to one hour of homework
- *Substantial:* An hour or more of homework

3. WHAT IS YOUR GROUP'S BIBLE KNOWLEDGE?

- *Beginner:* Group is comprised mostly of women who are new to the Bible or who don't feel confident in their Bible knowledge.
- *Intermediate:* Group has some experience with studying the Bible, and they have some familiarity with the stories in the Bible.
- *Advanced:* Group is comfortable with the Bible, and can handle the challenge of searching the Scriptures for themselves.

4. WHAT FORMAT DO YOU PREFER?

- *Print and Video:* Watch a Bible teacher on video, followed by a facilitated discussion.
- *Print Only:* Have the group leader give a short talk and lead a discussion of a study guide or a book.

Get Started!

Plug your answers into the Bible Study Finder, and discover the studies that best fit your group!

Check out Bible Study Finder at:
BibleStudySourcForWomen.com